Leading in Your Youth Group

John C. Maxwell
Leadership Books for Students

(Based on *Developing the Leader Within You*)

Leading from the Lockers:	*Leading from the Lockers:*
Student Edition	*Guided Journal*
ISBN 0-8499-7722-3	ISBN 0-8499-7723-1

The PowerPak Series

Leading Your Sports Team	*Leading in Your Youth Group*
ISBN 0-8499-7725-8	ISBN 0-8499-7726-6
Leading at School	*Leading As a Friend*
ISBN 0-8499-7724-X	ISBN 0-8499-7727-4

"These books are outstanding. John Maxwell's leadership principles have been communicated in a way that any student can understand and practice. Take them and go make a difference in your world."

—Dr. Tim Elmore,
Vice President of Leadership Development, EQUIP;
Author of *Nurturing the Leader in Your Child*

Leading in Your Youth Group

by

John C. Maxwell

with

Mark Littleton

TOMMY NELSON®
Thomas Nelson, Inc. • Nashville

POWERPAK SERIES: LEADING IN YOUR YOUTH GROUP

Based on John C. Maxwell's *Developing the Leader Within You.*

Published in Nashville, Tennessee, by Tommy Nelson®, a division of Thomas Nelson, Inc.

Special thanks to Ron Luce and Teen Mania for providing research materials for this book.

Unless otherwise indicated, Scripture quotations are from the *International Children's Bible, New Century Version*, copyright © 1983, 1986, 1988.

Library of Congress Cataloging-in-Publication Data

Maxwell, John C., 1947–
　　　Leading in your youth group / originated by John C. Maxwell;
　　adapted by Mark Littleton.
　　　　p. cm.
　　　ISBN 0-8499-7726-6
　　　1. Christian Leadership.　2. Youth—Religious life.　I. Littleton, Mark R.,
　　1950–　II. Title.

BV652.1 .M367 2001
259'.23—dc21

2001030960

Printed in the United States of America

01 02 03 04 05 PHX 5 4 3 2 1

Contents

1
Me Lead?

Being a leader isn't easy. Remember Moses? When God called him at the burning bush in Exodus 3, what did Moses do? He offered every excuse in the book to get out of it.

But God knew better. He knew not only what Moses was—a failed deliverer of Israel who was now herding sheep—but what Moses would become—one of the greatest leaders in history. Moses had the right stuff.

What kind of leader is God molding *you* to become?

Leading with Style

You might think, I DON'T HAVE THE RIGHT SKILLS! *I can't even talk in front of a group.*

Everyone finds these things difficult at first. It's a matter of trying them and not giving up when things get tough.

I think of Paco. Not someone you'd immediately consider a leader, he still attended the usual youth group functions. On an overnight retreat in which several non-Christians were invited by their Christian friends, the groups all went out hiking. They left their food near their tents. When they returned an animal had gotten into their food, and one of the groups **had nothing left to eat** or drink.

No one had brought very much food for the brief trip, and there wasn't a way to get more. Paco asked his group if they'd like to share. They agreed.

GOD DOESN'T CHOOSE GREAT LEADERS. HE CHOOSES GOOD PEOPLE WHOM HE MAKES INTO GREAT LEADERS.

Paco and his youth group approached the

other group and offered to share their food. As they ate and talked, the boys all became friends. At the end of the retreat, one of the visitors thanked Paco, saying, "I've never had time for that God stuff before, but I really like your group, and I'd like to be in a youth group like yours."

> "REACH UP AS FAR AS YOU CAN, AND GOD WILL REACH DOWN ALL THE WAY."
>
> —JOHN H. VINCENT, AMERICAN BISHOP

Paco was amazed that his simple act could have such long-term results. The next week, the youth pastor decided to have Paco give testimony at the youth meeting. Paco found it a thrill to stand up in front of the youth group to tell "his story" and what happened on the retreat. The kids laughed at his jokes and teared up as he voiced his commitment to Christ and how his *small act of kindness* had changed another's life. Gradually, he moved into positions of leadership to help build a fine youth group.

If God wants you to step in and make peace or lead in some other way, He'll give you the resources you need.

Be a Mentor

Whom do you look up to most? Whom would you most like to be like?

If you said leaders in your youth group, in your church, and those who speak up for Christ in the community, you'd be following people who are most likely worthy to be your mentors.

But you, too, could be a mentor. A leader.

Jesus plans to make you like Him by turning you into a fisher, not of fish, but of people. He wants you to go out into the world and lead people to Christ, bring them into God's kingdom, and teach them how to act, live, and speak as Jesus did—with holiness, godliness, and love. How do you do that? You lead by example. By being a good example of Christian

MATTHEW 20:25–26: YOU KNOW THAT THE RULERS OF THE NON-JEWISH PEOPLE LOVE TO SHOW THEIR POWER OVER THE PEOPLE. AND THEIR IMPORTANT LEADERS LOVE TO USE ALL THEIR AUTHORITY. BUT IT SHOULD NOT BE THAT WAY AMONG YOU. IF ONE OF YOU WANTS TO BECOME GREAT, THEN HE MUST SERVE THE REST OF YOU LIKE A SLAVE.

values, you are more likely to find your friends in and out of the youth group listening to you.

God may not call you to be a pastor or missionary, but He might ask you to put in time as a leader your friends will follow at meetings and worship retreats, on mission trips, and in everyday life.

You can never count yourself out. God often picked people who didn't look like leaders at all when He summoned them: Moses, Joshua, Elijah, Elisha, and others. These people all became great leaders because God had called them and given them His complete support.

Your Christian Walk

- will help you become more like Jesus (Romans 8:29)
- will make those you lead want to hear your Christian testimony (2 Timothy 4:2–5)
- will give you a chance to grow and help others (1 Timothy 4:16)
- will open closed doors (Revelation 3:8)

What Would You Do?

Imagine you're on a mission trip with your youth group. Everyone is excited; the bus echoes with strong, happy, laughing voices as your friends talk about what will happen the next day. You notice one of the guys says little and sits sullenly in a backseat. People seem to be avoiding him.

He's the pastor's son, known somewhat for his rejection of all things Christian. He said he's on this trip only because his dad made him go.

Various thoughts zip through your mind as you glance backward:

So what? He's a jerk. Let him be.

I've tried to talk to him. He just brushes everyone off.

Give him one more try.

You fight off that last inner impulse, but deep down you sense it's the voice of God.

2 TIMOTHY 2:2: YOU AND MANY OTHERS HAVE HEARD WHAT I HAVE TAUGHT. YOU SHOULD TEACH THE SAME THING TO SOME PEOPLE YOU CAN TRUST. THEN THEY WILL BE ABLE TO TEACH IT TO OTHERS.

Would you go and try to talk to him?

Most youth groups have their "forced" members, young people who are not there voluntarily but under orders from their moms or dads. Getting close to such people and winning them over call for real leadership. Someone to step in, speak the right words, and wield influence to move them from rung 1 to rung 2 on the ladder to Christian commitment.

How could you win a "forced" member over?

☐ When asked by youth pastors to lead, try it.

☐ Try to find a subject or hobby that interests both of you.

☐ Talk to her.

☐ Listen to her.

☐ Ask her opinions.

☐ Be sure to always greet her in a positive manner.

☐ Include her in activities—even outside the church.

It won't happen overnight, but eventually you'll win the member over. Guess what? These same tips work with new members.

Young people who became great leaders for Christ:

- **David**—after slaying Goliath, he went on to become Israel's greatest king.

- **Esther**—she risked her life to save the Jewish people.

- **Mark**—he deserted Paul and Barnabas on one of their journeys, but later Paul referred to him as "invaluable."

- **Mary Magdalene**—she was converted by Jesus and became the first one to tell the world Jesus had risen from the dead.

- **Timothy**—his mother and grandmother led him to Christ, then Paul led him into leadership.

Develop Leadership Muscles

How do you begin to develop your leadership abilities?

- ☐ Keep reading this book.
- ☐ Daily apply the principles you're learning.
- ☐ When asked by youth pastors to lead, try it.
- ☐ Talk to God about your fears and ask Him to help you overcome them.

JOHN 4:23: THE TIME IS COMING WHEN THE TRUE WORSHIPERS WILL WORSHIP THE FATHER IN SPIRIT AND TRUTH. THAT TIME IS NOW HERE. AND THESE ARE THE KINDS OF WORSHIPERS THE FATHER WANTS.

As you develop your leadership skills, others will notice. And sooner or later, if you prove you can complete the little things, God will give you bigger things (Matthew 25:21). One day, you may be the one who gets to speak to thousands at a rally because you were faithful each little step along the way.

Be on the lookout. When God taps you on the shoulder, don't flinch. Instead, accept the challenge and do your best.

2
Influence:
The Way to Lead

What is leadership? Leadership is *influence*.

For instance, Keiko watched her friend Brigit lead a group discussion one Sunday night at Breakaway, their youth group. Keiko noticed that Brigit tended to dominate the discussion and answer her own questions. After the meeting, KEIKO STOPPED BRIGIT in the hall. "Hey, I think I have some suggestions for you in leading discussion groups," she said.

"Really?" Brigit answered. "What should I do?"

Keiko offered Brigit a couple of suggestions. The next Sunday, Keiko overheard people in

Brigit's group talking. She noticed Brigit wasn't dominating as before. Brigit had taken Keiko's advice!

That's influence. When you can make a comment or offer an idea that changes someone's behavior, you are not only influencing that person, you're leading him.

You Gotta Have Followers to Be a Leader!

To be a leader, you must have followers. To lead means you have someone behind you saying, "Lead on, we're with you!"

Well, something like that.

So how do you get followers? Through influence. As you act out your faith in all you do, relate your ideas to your youth group, or share your faith with nonbelievers, YOU'RE INFLUENCING OTHERS, whether you realize it or not.

For instance, Elise had been a member of a youth group for years and rarely spoke up. But when she did, she often impressed everyone with her common sense and cool-headed brilliance.

When election time came around during her senior year, Debi asked Elise to run for president of the group. "Me—president?" Elise said. "You've got to be kidding. I've never been the head of or president of anything."

"But you're the best," Debi said. "You always know what to do. That's what we need."

Elise, though quiet, had subtly exercised influence merely by being sensible and collected when problems arose.

How Do You Influence Others?

- By sending a note that says, "I appreciated what you did."
- By providing a pat on the back or hug.
- By cheering them on.
- By giving helpful suggestions, when asked.
- By offering encouragement.
- By setting a good example.
- By standing against the tide when going with the tide is wrong.
- By being calm when others panic.

Are You Ready to Lead?

Todd wanted to use his influence to lead others, but no one really thought of him as a leader. He was okay-looking, but not popular. He had good ideas, but they either weren't taken seriously or didn't fly. He prayed about being a leader. He studied good leaders.

Then **Todd realized he wasn't ready** to be a leader. He practiced his speaking and teaching on the little kids in a children's Bible study class his mother taught. He did everything he could to prepare to be a good leader. And he wondered when God would choose him to lead.

One day the pastor asked Todd to give his testimony in church. Todd had never done that, but he worked hard and prepared a five-minute testimony. He practiced in front of a mirror, with his friends, and with his family, and ultimately he presented his testimony to the church.

Afterward, people were very complimentary. **"Great job!"** One of the elders said, "We need more youth like you." And the youth pastor asked, "Hey, Todd, how about giving your testimony at our rally next week? We'll have a lot of kids there who are unbelievers."

Todd did just that. And ever since, God has put him into more leadership roles. Todd got ready, and God gave him an opportunity.

Is Your Influence Good or Bad?

You will always influence others. The question is, will your influence be good or bad? You've probably influenced someone for good and maybe for bad, too. Think about it. Did you ever talk someone into **breaking a rule?** Or talk someone into *keeping* a rule? If so, you influenced that person.

You never know when you are influencing someone. For example, a new Christian hung around one of the youth group leaders, trying to learn how to walk more closely with Jesus. The new Christian was a TRACK STAR. One night the leader invited him to a party. There, the new Christian watched, amazed, as the leader chugged a beer and then had several others. When he asked the leader about it, the leader said, "Ahhh, I wouldn't do it at church, but no one'll know, so what's the big deal?"

The new Christian thought, *Hey, why not?* Then he promptly got drunk, too. That night, while driving himself home, he had a wreck that was his fault. In the accident, he injured himself, others, and totaled his father's car—his dad's only way to get to work. On top of that, he broke his leg and couldn't compete in track meets the rest of the year, which caused him to lose a scholarship to college. His whole life changed because he followed a bad leader and made a bad decision.

Paul told the Corinthians not to follow a bad example. But some people won't recognize someone as a bad example until they get into trouble.

Be careful what kind of influence you're having on others. God will call you into account for anyone you lead into sin.

If You Catch One, Don't Throw Him Back!

Today, if you ever attend a fishing competition, you will find that after hooking a great fish, the competitors usually throw the fish back into the water. That's because they want to preserve the fish and the environment.

But in leadership, when you hook a follower, by no means throw him back. You want to train him or her, help him or her grow closer to God, and be a good influence on others, so they, too, can become fishers of people for God.

1 JOHN 4:18: WHERE GOD'S LOVE IS, THERE IS NO FEAR, BECAUSE GOD'S PERFECT LOVE TAKES AWAY FEAR.

If you're like me, you probably want to build God's kingdom and be part of bringing lost people into God's kingdom. If that's so, then remember that leadership (fishing) is a serious business. To lose someone you're leading is to lose a soul. Think about how you're influencing others and make sure it's for good, for God, and for the truth, not like the "drinking" leader.

Start Where You Are

How does one become an influential leader? There are different levels of leadership. You can be a leader by *position* because the pastor says, "I want you to lead the group today." You can be a leader by *permission* because your youth group says, "We value your ideas, and we want you to lead us." You can be a leader by *production* because everyone says, "We believe you will get us where we want to go with this project."

THE BEST LEADERS LEAD BY PRODUCTION, but almost everyone begins leading by position or appointment. For example, you become the leader because the pastor or youth pastor or someone else says, "You're it. Go and do it." This often happens in smaller youth groups where many members are not very committed. They need a leader, but no one has emerged. The

"LET NO MAN IMAGINE THAT HE HAS NO INFLU-ENCE. WHOEVER HE MAY BE, AND WHER-EVER HE MAY BE PLACED, THE MAN WHO THINKS BECOMES A LIGHT AND A POWER."
—HENRY GEORGE, POLITICAL ECONOMIST

pastor simply designates someone as the leader.

When **YOU'RE APPOINTED A LEADER,** there can be real problems. The biggest one is that others in your youth group will follow you because the pastor says they have to fol-low. They're not doing it out of love, respect, or commitment. That's why appointed lead-ers sometimes have a hard time getting people to do their assigned jobs. But you

Tamasha—Appointed Leadership

Tamasha was the pastor's daughter, and she generally took over everything. Because of her relation to the pastor, she was often appointed leader by the youth pastor or the teachers. But few of the kids really liked her or her style. One day at school, Tamasha realized none of the kids from the youth group hung around with her. She asked someone why and they said, "Why should we?"

It was then that Tamasha realized she couldn't lead just because someone said she was the leader, but she had to "win" others' approval. She did this by helping others, tutoring several who wanted to learn guitar, and, in general, being an encourager. It was then that the kids started to respect and like her as a person. She had moved from a leader by position to a leader by permission.

don't have to stay a leader by appointment; you can rise to being a leader by production through following the goals in this book.

The Three Levels of Leadership

POSITION—the pastor says, "I want you all to give so-and-so your attention. He's going to lead us today."

PERMISSION—the youth group says, "You've got good ideas. We want to follow you."

PRODUCTION—everyone says, "We believe you will get us where we need to go because you've done so many good things. Lead on!"

Lead On!

When you demonstrate that you care about people by doing acts of kindness and goodness, they will care about you. They will believe you know your stuff, and they've seen

Roger—Leadership by Permission

Brett was elected president of the debate club, and Roger a vice president, which was fine with Roger. As president, though, Brett didn't perform as others thought he would. Once he reached president, he thought he wouldn't have much to do and could goof off, and he wasn't getting the job done. But when you're the president, you have lots of work to do. Roger, as vice president, saw tasks "slipping through the cracks," and he stepped in and began making sure things were done. He organized several guys to put away the chairs after each meeting. He got a couple of girls and guys to provide and organize snacks, and he planned out the meetings. The following year, Roger was voted president, and Brett wasn't elected to an office. It wasn't a popularity contest. The youth "permitted" Roger to be their leader because he had won their confidence and approval.

that you're good at what you do. Thus, they will heartily give you permission to lead. They'll say, "We will follow you because you have won our allegiance."

Top Dog

The level to aspire to in leadership is the one I call *production*. At this level, the leader makes things happen, gets the group going in the right direction, and starts accomplishing something. Attitudes improve. People join in willingly. The youth group starts to grow, and everyone's amazed.

But it could all go back to one person who, with God's help, started to produce results. He made things happen. For example, Roger began leading by permission (he was elected by the group), but he then went on to lead by production (he made things happen).

I believe this should be

1 TIMOTHY 4:12: YOU ARE YOUNG, BUT DO NOT LET ANYONE TREAT YOU AS IF YOU WERE NOT IMPORTANT. BE AN EXAMPLE TO SHOW THE BELIEVERS HOW THEY SHOULD LIVE.

Jesus—Leadership by Production

Jesus is the classic example of One who led on all three levels. At His baptism, God's voice resounded, "This is My beloved Son in whom I am well pleased."

That was position.

As Jesus went out into the world and gained respect through His miracles and words, various disciples joined Him. They did this willingly. They even attempted to do the kinds of things Jesus did—heal, cast out demons, and walk on water. They followed Jesus because they were committed to Him personally.

That was permission.

As Jesus' words showed their spiritual power, as He amazed everyone with His deeds, as He spoke of God's plan to save all people, gave hope, and changed lives, His disciples saw Him as a leader they would die for. He produced, and for this His followers were willing to give everything.

the goal of every leader. Often, leadership starts
with position or permission, but if you get the
group's permission and start to produce, you
become a genuine leader,
the kind young people
will follow gladly and
even wholeheartedly.

What kind of leader are
you?

Don't worry if you real-
ize that your leadership role is largely based on
position at this point. Everyone has to start
somewhere. Keep reading for more tips on
leadership.

HEBREWS 13:5:
GOD HAS SAID, "I
WILL NEVER LEAVE
YOU; I WILL NEVER
FORGET YOU."

3
Focus, Focus, Focus

Have you ever played "Pin the Tail on the Donkey"? It's a game in which a blindfolded player tries to pin the tail on a paper donkey's backside, but instead the players usually end up pinning the tail to lampshades, mirrors, distant walls, and even other kids (well, almost).

The most important elements of leadership are priorities and goal-setting, but if you become blinded by other things, you'll end up pinning the goal on the wrong thing—just like the game above. When you create a goal that the group wants to reach—say attracting six new members in six months—that's what you point toward. Don't go around pinning tails on other things like having the most cookouts or going on field trips. Keep focused on your goal and the steps it takes to reach it.

Take the goal above: six new members in six months. That's not an unusual goal for a youth group to have. What does making that goal a priority do for your youth group?

IT MOTIVATES EVERYONE. And when that first, second, and third person join, excitement builds. "Hey, we're going to get all our new members and maybe more." "This is the best we ever did." "Man, we should go for ten new members the next six months!"

People get excited when they see goals being reached.

If you want to lead others, one of your main jobs will be to set goals and then think up steps to reach those goals. As you learn to set goals and the steps to reach them, you'll be ahead of most leaders out there.

Climbing Mountains

The way to start reaching your youth group's goals is by prioritizing your day, your week, even your year. What things are most important for you to accomplish today? (Maybe your goal is to study for a test, clean your room, save money for a gift, graduate to the next grade.) One of the best ways to do this is to make a list. What goals do you have for today? What really matters to you and your youth group?

For instance, consider some of the goals God has for you as an individual believer:

- ☐ Convert you to faith in Christ (John 1: 12)
- ☐ Develop you into a disciple (Matthew 28:18–20)
- ☐ Enable you to teach and help others (2 Timothy 2:2)
- ☐ Transform you so you become like Jesus in character (Romans 8:29)
- ☐ Get you to His eternal kingdom so you can live with Him forever (John 14:1–3; Revelation 3:21)

Now look at those goals. If those are what God wants to do in your life, what kinds of goals should you have in the life of your youth group? Try these on for size:

1. To lead other young people to Christ (Perhaps put a number and time frame on it.)

2. To train those converts in the basics of the faith

3. To help them become a little more like Jesus

See how quickly biblical goals can become the goals of the group?

Order or Disorder?

One of the first ways to prioritize is to get your life in order. Get organized. From your bedroom to your locker, think about having things organized so you can find them when you need them.

In the same way, a youth group needs to get

organized so it can flex its muscles and get out there and achieve things for God's kingdom.

Organizing is rather simple. Start with a piece of paper you can keep with you at all times. Maybe an index card. Brainstorm with other members of your group at a meeting. List all the things you and they think you'd like to see happen in your group for that month or that year. Don't prioritize yet; simply list everything you can think of that your group wants to do.

You can do this with yourself and your own life, too. In fact, it's a good idea to practice prioritizing on your own before you take it to the group.

Once you've created a list, select the three to five most important activities or plans and start working on them together. Say your list looks like this:

☐ Talk to one new person about Christ every week.

☐ Invite one new person each month to a youth meeting.

☐ Memorize one new Bible verse each week.

☐ Read the Bible every day.

☐ Listen to one good CD, tape, or video each week.

☐ Clean up the youth group's area or church grounds, etc.

☐ Appoint three people to be responsible for making sure there is food at meetings.

Now look at the list. Which ones are most important? Least important? Number them in the order you need to do them, starting with the ones you need to do right away:

1. Talk to one new person about Christ every week.

5. Invite one new person each month to a youth meeting.

4. Memorize one new Bible verse each week.

3. Read the Bible every day.

7. Listen to one good CD, tape, or video each week.

6. Clean up the youth group's area, church grounds, etc.

2. Appoint three people to be responsible for making sure there is food at meetings. (Figures!)

EPHESIANS 5:17: SO DO NOT BE FOOLISH WITH YOUR LIVES. BUT LEARN WHAT THE LORD WANTS YOU TO DO.

Now study the list. Suddenly, you are organized! You and your group have some goals to go after.

More than that, you now have a pathway that will make your life easier and more fun. You will actually achieve something important today and may just enjoy doing it!

Priority Power

This all means that you're making choices. If you don't plan your own priorities, you'll soon be forced into doing what others want you to do.

Think about it: Your teacher, Sunday school teacher, and minister do this every week. They set goals for the week, month, and year, then figure out what steps need to be taken to reach those goals. Through their guidance each group makes progress toward all of its goals.

SOUNDS AWESOME. But guess what? You've probably already learned to set individual priorities! You do it in school and with your Bible lessons, by studying when you'd rather be

> "NOTHING IS PARTICU-LARLY HARD, IF YOU DIVIDE IT INTO SMALL JOBS."
> —HENRY FORD,
> BUSINESSMAN AND CREATOR
> OF ASSEMBLY-LINE METHODS

with your friends or listening to music or watching TV. And by setting priorities, look how much you've learned by the end of each year. Did you **reach your goal** of going to the next level? Most of the time, you probably did.

When you lead, you're setting priorities for the group to work as a team to reach a goal. Your youth group feels a lot of great things when they achieve those goals:

☐ **A sense of accomplishment**

☐ **Joy in Christ**

☐ A sense of vision

☐ They're part of a team

☐ That you're a good leader

Those are the kinds of things all leaders want to produce in the lives of their followers.

Sharing Every Day

What if you decided to give your group and yourself a significant goal like this one: Talk to at least one person every day about Jesus. It doesn't have to be a complete gospel presentation, but just that you "nudge" someone in the direction of faith by words from the Bible, your testimony, or some other source.

In the nineteenth century, one man made that his goal. His name was Dwight Moody. He was the Billy Graham of his day, preaching to millions of people, and leading millions more to Christ. He is credited with starting Moody Bible Institute, *Moody* magazine, Moody Church (a large church in Chicago), and the beginnings of the student organizations that have become Youth for Christ, Campus Life, Young Life, and InterVarsity. It's said that one night he was about to go to bed when he suddenly cried, "I haven't witnessed to anyone personally today!" He immediately put on his coat and went out and found someone to witness to.

Although it doesn't take a lot of time, this daily goal could change the world. Imagine if every Christian tried to live up to it. We'd turn the world upside down!

God's Will

There comes a point when every Christian has asked: What does God want me to do with my life? You won't answer this in one day; it may take a long time. You'll need to think about it and pray about it. But to help you decide, ask yourself a few questions:

☐ What does the Bible say about what I want to do? Are there any verses or truths I can use in support?

☐ What about prayer? Have I spent time asking God to lead me?

☐ Have I listened to God's answer, even if it's not what I want to hear?

☐ What do my parents, family, mentors, and friends say about it? What advice do they have?

☐ Do my circumstances indicate God is behind this?

When you seek to accomplish God's will in your life, you will be seeking the best and greatest things you could ever achieve. God wants what is best for you, what is most in line with your gifts and abilities, and what is clearly the purpose He has planned for your life.

Tim Seeks God's Will

One day as Tim sat in youth group listening to a speaker talk about knowing God's will, he prayed, *God, what do You want me to do with my life?*

Tim thought about this and prayed daily about it. He had considered the possibility of **being a pastor, a missionary, a doctor, or a lawyer**. But none of those professions much appealed to him.

The funny thing was, Tim was great at baking things. He created the most amazing cakes and pies for the youth group functions. One day he realized, "You know, I really like doing this. Could God want me to be a baker or a chef?"

PSALM 1:1: HAPPY IS THE PERSON WHO DOESN'T LISTEN TO THE WICKED. HE DOESN'T GO WHERE SINNERS GO. HE DOESN'T DO WHAT BAD PEOPLE DO.

He prayed in that direction. When he graduated from high school, he went on to a school for bakers where he learned to do even better than he'd ever imagined.

Don't think God will automatically call you into the ministry or put you into some church-related job. God's will covers a multitude of occupations and life's work. He can just as easily lead you into being an auto mechanic, nurse, or teacher, as being the next Billy Graham!

4
Living the Truth

Ken and Elaine were talking one day about Jim, who had just spent thirty minutes telling the youth group everything he wanted to do as their new leader.

"I think it's great Jim wants to do all those things," Ken said, "but I don't think they will happen."

"Why not?" Elaine asked.

"Jim likes everyone else to do all these things, but he can't even make time for them in his own life! He says one thing, then does something else."

Elaine nodded. "It's a problem."

"I just wish someone would become president

whose life matches his words," Ken said. "Someone I could follow."

"I'm going to pray for Jim," Elaine said.

What Are You Shouting?

Have you ever heard the expression "What you are shouts so loud that I can't hear what you say"?

That's the issue above. Jim talked big, but he accomplished little. Maybe his heart wasn't in it. Maybe he preferred boasting. Maybe he didn't know how to do the things he dreamed about.

1 TIMOTHY 4:16: BE CAREFUL IN YOUR LIFE AND IN YOUR TEACHING. CONTINUE TO LIVE AND TEACH RIGHTLY. THEN YOU WILL SAVE YOURSELF AND THOSE PEOPLE WHO LISTEN TO YOU.

Most of all, it was an issue of integrity. What's integrity? It's living up to what you say to others. YOU CAN SHOUT all you want about goals, priorities, and building God's kingdom, but if you lie, cheat, steal, gossip, hate, exhibit racism or bigotry, or do any number of other wrongs, you will never lead. People do not follow someone they can't believe in and trust.

TRUST: That's the issue. How do you get people to trust you?

Through integrity. By doing what is right every time. If you do bungle it (or even sin), then you confess it, ask for forgiveness, and move on.

Honesty isn't just the best policy. It's the *only* policy. If we're honest every time, we will win the admiration and commitment of others around us. Integrity is not so much what we do as who we are, for who we are determines what we do.

WWJD?

How do you become a person of integrity—a person of truthfulness? It's an essential quality for leadership in any group, but especially a youth group. Other group members are looking to you as an example of what Christ would do. You've probably seen "WWJD—What Would Jesus Do?" If you're a known Christian,

Bible Leaders Who Influenced Others

- David was a mighty leader in the Bible. At the end of his life, there were thirty "mighty men" who followed him (see list in 2 Samuel 23:8–39). David's good example had rubbed off.
- Moses was one of the greatest leaders in human history. His style and humility were so obvious that Joshua followed him to the letter. And Joshua also became a great leader in history.
- Paul influenced Timothy and Titus to become great church leaders.
- Jesus is the greatest example of a leader. He touched lepers, listened to questioners and tried to help them, reached out to people who were rejected and hated, even washed the disciples' feet on one occasion to show them how to be servants (see John 13), and His ministry continues through His followers two thousand years later.

people will measure you by that standard. Are you living up to what Jesus would do, or do you practice things—drinking, smoking, using drugs, swearing, cheating, stealing—that Jesus most assuredly wouldn't do?

For example, Jim (in the earlier story) was a great talker, but apparently he didn't get things done. PEOPLE COULDN'T TRUST HIM to do what he said he would do. What if Jim began making the goals of the youth group his personal goals for each day? What if other members saw him doing the things he talked about? That would build trust and create a reputation for integrity. Definitely.

Mirror, Mirror on the Wall... Is the Image You See Who You Really Are?

Today, people talk much about "image." How do people see you?

Consider politicians. They spend a lot of time and money projecting a certain image. But if it is a false image, that image will be shattered by the truth as easily as a rock breaks a mirror. Read the papers, watch the news. How many people's images are ruined—their reputations in tatters—

because of their own lying, dodging, and pretending? And what remains? A crippled leader.

Don't try to **project an image** that's not who you really are. It's much easier to be a person of integrity—to be a person of truthfulness.

One of my favorite stories is of a lad on crutches who was waiting for a subway. He had a host of Christmas packages balanced under his arms. The subway stopped, and everyone rushed to get on. The boy was trampled in the crush, sending his presents and crutches in all directions.

> "INTEGRITY HAS NO NEED FOR RULES."
> —ALBERT CAMUS,
> FRENCH-ALGERIAN
> PHILOSOPHER

A man saw the boy SPRAWLED OUT and ran over to help him gather up his things. As the man helped him onto the crowded subway, the boy looked into his face and asked, "Sir, are you Jesus?"

"No," the man replied. "But I'm one of His followers."

A follower who lives up to the truth of Jesus will go far to make others believe Jesus is worth following. On the other hand, a

Christian who is a bad example can do equally bad damage.

Do You Help Whenever You Can?

What if, when circumstances permitted, you . . .

- **helped** a hurting person by doing chores for him?
- **gave** your money to spread the message of Christ and help needy people?
- **spent** time in prayer for others?
- **took** the time to write a note and thank the people in your youth group who have done well?
- **showed** appreciation to a fellow student who did a good job?

Would you be doing what Jesus did?

The Game of Life

Sometimes people cater to a certain group to be popular or to get their way—even if it's not the best thing for the group. It's called "playing politics." Such people fall short in the integrity department. They're the ones who will run down other group members when the leaders aren't looking. They'll tell you all the reasons you shouldn't do what the group wants but do what these people want instead. They'll pretend to be Christian when in reality their goal is merely popularity or a certain position.

> ROMANS 13:8: DO NOT OWE PEOPLE ANYTHING. BUT YOU WILL ALWAYS OWE LOVE TO EACH OTHER.

Gayle was like that. She wanted to be a group leader, but to get the position, she played politics. She went around to each member, found out what he or she wanted, figured out how many things she could promise to get his or her support, and then asked for that person's vote.

A true leader, though, will try to offer solutions that meet everyone's need, and be honest if a solution is not available. A true leader will not go for just the need of the moment, but for the needs of the future.

Real integrity means doing what's right even if it's unpopular.

Being Lost Is Worse than Being Unpopular

Make a resolution that you can follow every day for the rest of your life: "I will do all I can to live the truth, not just talk about it."

If you do that, you will be a leader worth following. You will be on the inside who you are on the outside.

5
Change Makes Things Happen

Most people resist change. Rarely do we want to move from a comfortable, happy situation to an uncomfortable, weird one. We want things to remain as they are. "I liked it the way it was!" is a common statement. Yet often you will have no say in the matter. It will happen with you or without you.

So, how do you make a change that's out of your control into a change that's positive for the lives of those in your youth group? There are several ways. To start: Decide you will work with the change and be part of it, not fight it.

Turning Change into a Charge

Louis's church experienced a deep disruption. After about two years, Louis's youth director, Wade, like most youth directors, decided to take on a bigger job in another church. Louis had really liked Wade. He'd liked things the way they were.

The new youth director, Greta, was married to a seminary student. She had fuzzy hair, funny lipstick, and weird ideas. Louis believed she must have been hired only because no one else applied for the job.

One day, Louis was grumbling to his mother about the latest thing the new youth director wanted to do: take some people to Russia to work at building a new church there. His mother listened and then said, "You've never given Greta a chance."

"She doesn't deserve one!" Louis snapped back.

> HEBREWS 12:1: SO LET US RUN THE RACE THAT IS BEFORE US AND NEVER GIVE UP. WE SHOULD REMOVE FROM OUR LIVES ANYTHING THAT WOULD GET IN THE WAY. AND WE SHOULD REMOVE THE SIN THAT SO EASILY CATCHES US.

"And why is that?"

"She was only hired because she's the only one who applied."

"Louis, dozens of people applied for that position. She was hired because she's very good."

For the first time, Louis really thought about Greta. Finally, he stammered, "Well, **SHE'S NOT LiKE WADE!"**

"So, Greta's different. She teaches differently than Wade did. It doesn't make one better or worse.

> "YOU CAN TURN PAINFUL SITUATIONS AROUND THROUGH LAUGHTER. IF YOU CAN FIND HUMOR IN ANYTHING—EVEN POVERTY—YOU CAN SURVIVE IT."
>
> —**BiLL COSBY,** ENTERTAINER

It just makes them different. It's our differences that make the world interesting. If we were all the same, the world would be boring. I think God put this youth director in your life for a reason. God is giving you a chance to see the way other people serve Christ. Your attitude is keeping you from following God's will. Why don't you give her a chance and follow her for a while. Isn't that what Jesus would say to do?"

Louis thought about it and decided to

change his attitude and try to work with the new youth director. He became a leader in the youth group. He went to Russia, and it turned his life around. He became a committed disciple of Christ.

That can take place if you decide to let the change happen and flow with it.

Change Can Be a Gift

Most people work with change on a daily basis. New teachers. New coaches. New schools.

For those in a church youth group, the changes can be even greater. What if your old group was . . .

☐ large

☐ fun

☐ had lots of friends you'd known since grade school

☐ and had a great youth pastor

But the new one is . . .

☐ **small**

☐ **has all new people**

☐ **and has no youth pastor, just a young couple who, you think, aren't exactly "cool"**

It can turn your life upside down.

John and James

In the New Testament, we find that these two brothers were called the "sons of thunder." Why? Because they were always wanting to call down lightning bolts on anyone who didn't agree with them.

Jesus worked with them, and in time they began to grow. John ended up writing five books of the New Testament—John, 1 John, 2 John, 3 John, and Revelation. His brother, James, was the first great leader of the Church and also its first martyr.

These were two guys who found that changing wasn't hard, once you let Jesus take charge.

Sooner or later you'll ask yourself: Am I really satisfied with my world like it is? Can I do better? Would I like to go for broke? Would I like to accomplish all God has in mind for me?

If so, then change is the way God will do it.

Trusting Change

As a youth leader, how do you help your group with change? First, start by trusting others. Believe in them. Have confidence they will respond with as much enthusiasm as you, once they understand what needs to happen.

EPHESIANS 5:18: DO NOT BE DRUNK WITH WINE. THAT WILL RUIN YOU SPIRITUALLY. BUT BE FILLED WITH THE SPIRIT.

Second, be sure you're ready for the change and are willing to change yourself, if necessary. You can't expect people to want to do something you aren't willing to do yourself.

Change is what life is all about. God wants us to change from rebels to believers, from sinners to saints.

Where are you in that process? Are you letting Him change you?

Peter the Mistake Maker

Peter was the classic leader: always charging ahead, not thinking about what was really happening around him. One day his best friend, Jesus, came to him and his friends on a lake. Jesus happened to be walking on water. What did Peter do? He jumped out of the boat and said, "Let me do it, too." He walked a little way out there, and it was great. But then he looked up at the wind and waves and promptly sank. Jesus had to pull him out.

When Jesus was about to go to the cross, Peter whipped out a sword and cut off someone's ear. He just wasn't a very good aim. Jesus healed the guy's ear, then told Peter to put the sword away because he was going to make some big mistakes that night. Later on, Peter wouldn't even own up to being Jesus' friend. When people asked him if he was one of Jesus' disciples, he denied it. Three times.

Peter went home and wept.

But God had other things in mind. After Jesus rose from the dead, He got Peter going the right way. And at Peter's first sermon, three thousand people were converted. Peter did well because he changed from being an impetuous, feisty disciple to being a true follower of Jesus.

6
Tough Problem, Tougher Leader

We all have problems—big ones, little ones, medium-size ones. Leaders are problem-solvers. People follow a leader because they believe he or she can solve the problems they're facing. After all, why do we elect a president? To fix what's broken, and keep what's right going right.

The good news is that it's not all up to you to fix everything. As a Christian, you have the greatest problem-solver of all time inside you. Jesus solved the problems of death, sin, eternity, heaven, hell, and everything else, and you have His Spirit in your heart. So never feel you're out there alone on anything you do for Him.

He will always be available to you as you lead the youth in your group. Just as Moses saw the sea parted when he and all Israel were about to be killed, so YOU WILL SEE GREAT THINGS happen as you serve God. He still works incredible miracles.

Grow through Problem-Solving

What will solving problems give you as a youth leader?

- ☐ A chance to see God work in and through you
- ☐ The opportunity to grow spiritually
- ☐ The experience of God's power and wisdom
- ☐ Personal satisfaction in solving problems

You can see that you will become a better, stronger, wiser, and more resilient person through solving problems.

Problem-Solve with Emotional Support

Nicole's friend Sally came to her in tears. "My boyfriend broke up with me today," Sally said. "I'm so upset."

Nicole comforted her friend as best she could by hugging her, listening to her story, praying with her, and offering kind words of encouragement, like:

☐ *"There are other guys out there."*

☐ *"He doesn't deserve you!"*

☐ *"The guy's a fool to leave you."*

Well, maybe not those exact words, but something like them, except they were comforting.

A week later, Sally stopped Nicole in the hall. "You know, you really helped me last week," she said.

"How? I didn't do anything," Nicole said.

"Yes, you listened to me. You reminded me God was in control, and you prayed with me. That helped. A lot."

Sometimes it's the little problems that look so big that can be solved very easily—by kind words, strong wisdom, and loving encouragement.

Who Were the Great Problem-Makers of the Bible?

- Sarah—she persuaded her husband to mate with her handmaiden, which caused so much conflict, it still exists today in the fight between the Arabs and the Jews.

- Rebekah—she encouraged her son Jacob to steal from his brother Esau, causing more conflict.

- Samson—he was so proud and lustful, he ended up losing his life when Delilah learned how to defeat him.

- Moses—he killed an Egyptian taskmaster and then hid out for forty years.

- David—doing a forbidden census cost the lives of seventy thousand Jews.

God had to deal with people like this in getting His plan to take effect. How would you like that job?

Problems Are Opportunities in Disguise

I have used five basic steps in solving problems. They are:

1. Identify the problem. You've got to know what the problem is before you can fix anything.

2. Ask questions. Make sure you have the right problem to solve. Ask the questions that will zero in on what's really the matter.

3. Talk to people in the know about the problem. There is wisdom in getting many viewpoints, and it's wise to consult with others before running off to solve the wrong problem.

4. Make sure you have the facts. Study the situation and make sure you're sure what is wrong.

5. Try something to see if it works. Often, you may have to try several different ways of solving the problem before you hit on the right one. Consider Thomas Edison. He invented the light bulb, while others scoffed and said it couldn't be done. It took more than a year and ten thousand attempts. When asked about his progress, Edison replied, "We know ten thousand ways not to do it." But eventually he invented not only the light bulb, but the circuitry to light a city!

COLOSSIANS 3:16: LET THE TEACHING OF CHRIST LIVE IN YOU RICHLY. USE ALL WISDOM TO TEACH AND STRENGTHEN EACH OTHER.

You can use these problem-solving techniques to solve the tough situations that will arise in any youth group. I personally have seen it work many times in my church and my life.

Len's youth group was foundering. As the leader, Len was expected to fix things. So he set about using the problem-solving process on page 59. He zeroed in on the problem, asked the right questions, consulted with several people, and got the facts. In the end, they found out what the real problem was: One of the members in the group was such a gossip that no one felt free to open up to others in real ways for fear it would be told to everyone.

When Len realized this was the biggest cause

of all the other problems, he sat down and talked with the member, who confessed and made a public apology, and people began showing up. At first, people didn't trust the member, but he proved he could be trusted and had changed his ways.

> "REAL LEADERS ARE ORDINARY PEOPLE WITH EXTRAORDINARY DETERMINATIONS."
>
> **—JOHN SEAMAN GARRIS,**
> **AUTHOR**

All problems are not simple. But many have solutions that don't require the miraculous. Follow this process, and I guarantee you will see positive results.

7
A Leading Attitude

Your attitude will determine just about anything you do as a leader. The right attitude can take you far. The wrong one can sink you faster than the *Titanic*.

Consider some of the attitudes God wants to develop in you from the Bible:

The Key Christian Attitudes

☐ **Faithfulness** (Luke 16:10–12)—*doing the job*

☐ **Hopefulness** (Hebrews 11:1)—*keeping positive*

- ☐ **Forgiveness** (Matthew 18:22)—letting others off the hook

- ☐ **Love** (1 Corinthians 13:1–13)—reaching out and giving of yourself

- ☐ **Gentleness** (Galatians 5:22–23)—being easy on people

- ☐ **Kindness** (Galatians 5:22–23)—showing a friendly side

- ☐ **Peacefulness** (Romans 12:18)—maintaining a settled, joyous heart

- ☐ **Happiness** (Psalm 1:1–3)—being upbeat and glad

- ☐ **Endurance** (James 1:2–4)—hanging in there

Beware of Emotions

Emotions are very fleeting. They come and go. Sometimes they can't be trusted. To let emotional feelings run your life is like letting the weather determine whether you will wake up in the morning.

For instance, chances are some day you will

Power Attitude

Everyone in the youth group waxed ecstatic when they learned the youth were starting their own praise band. They found two guitarists, a pianist and organist, a drummer, and several singers. It looked great. Ted had been in bands before and knew about the grueling practices. At bass, he knew he wasn't a centerpiece of the band, but he bided his time. At one practice, the leader blew up over one of the guitarists failing to get a riff. At another, the drummer said he wanted to quit. All Ted said at each was, "Hang in there, the good stuff is coming."

At first, everyone laughed at Ted's words. But gradually, they realized Ted was the centerpiece of the band. His upbeat attitude kept everyone from flying off into anger or disgust.

At the end of the year, Ted was given an award for excellence. It said, "You and God kept us together. But without you, we might have forgotten about God." Ted has often said it was one of the great days in his life.

fall in love with someone. Those feelings will start off intense and beautiful. But they may fade. Most couples admit they have to "work at" their love or it will die.

> "LEADERSHIP IS PRAC-TICED NOT SO MUCH IN WORDS AS IN ATTITUDE AND IN ACTIONS."
> —HAROLD GENEEN, FOUNDER, MCI COMMUNICATIONS

Remember how enthusiastic you were about that new project you got involved in—maybe it was the praise band at church, a retreat or trip with the youth, or perhaps a course at school. Often, people start off with sails unfurled, ready for adventure. But then the grind sets in. It gets hard. All those wondrous feelings of adventure and excitement simmer down. Suddenly, you have to plod along at a snail's pace.

That's not the time to think you should give up. That's just an indication that you're learning to do a job despite the hardness of it.

Bad Attitude, Low Aptitude

The wrong attitude can run like wildfire through a youth group. Suddenly, because a few bad attitudes get heard, everyone grumbles, harps, and puts each other down.

But the right attitude will take everyone much further.

How do you get the right attitude fixed firmly in your mind? Below are some steps I've found to work:

1. Identify problem feelings.

Be aware of any bad attitudes. Drop them like a rock.

Ted (in the earlier story) didn't let others make him feel bad. He kept on sailing along, despite cold winds.

HEBREWS 12:2: LET US LOOK ONLY TO JESUS. HE IS THE ONE WHO BEGAN OUR FAITH, AND HE MAKES OUR FAITH PERFECT.

2. Identify problem behavior.

What are you doing wrong? If you don't know, ask your mother or father. You can be sure she or he will tell it to you straight.

At times, Ted talked to others about his own attitude. He got a fix on moments when he was down and learned to avoid talking at such instances.

3. Identify problem thinking.

What goes through your mind that you need to stop? *I'll never win; I'm a loser.* Refuse to think that way, or you will be that way forever.

When Ted first joined the band, he thought that because bass wasn't loud and raucous, he didn't matter that much. But one day he realized how bass put down a basic line for the band that can carry the group—and he realized he was important. He decided to focus on that rather than other negative thoughts that flitted into his head.

4. Identify right thinking.

When you do find some good, wholesome thoughts, work on strengthening them. Use those thoughts to your advantage.

Ted often concentrated on repeating Scriptures in his mind as he practiced with the band. This kept him on center.

5. Make a public commitment to right thinking.

Tell your youth group you're in a new frame of mind. It's win-or-die-trying for you from now on!

Ted did this every time he spoke up, though no one knew he was committing himself to positive thinking each time.

6. Develop a plan for right thinking.

Put it on paper. Put the paper in your wallet, a journal, or prayer list, and read it now and then.

Ted even wrote down some of his thoughts

Keeping Your Attitudes Right

- Say the right words—they encourage others.

- Read the right books—they feed your mind.

- Listen to the right tapes—they build you up.

- Be with the right people—they will pick you up when you're down.

- Do the right things—they reinforce you on your course.

- Pray the right prayers—they're the source of God's power.

Do all that, and your heart also will be right.

and Bible verses. He kept them in his pocket for ready reference.

Bad habits and bad attitudes are like acid. They not only eat away at your insides, but they will spew out and affect others.

Good attitudes are like clear, cold, fresh water. They refresh and revitalize everyone, including you.

8
Relationships:
The Fabric of Life

Relationships are what life is all about. And your relationship with God is key to everything. But right relationships with the people in your life, believers and unbelievers, will please God and move Him to strengthen you in other ways.

Think of how many relationships there are in the usual youth group:

- ☐ You and God
- ☐ You and yourself
- ☐ You and your family

☐ You and the youth pastor or youth leaders
☐ You and each of the other youth members
☐ You and the people in your small group
☐ You and the whole youth group
☐ You and the church
☐ You and the pastors and other major leaders

That can cover many relationships. Besides that, think of how different you can be with a best friend in contrast to being with the youth pastor or a new student. You don't talk about the same things. In many ways, YOU'RE NOT quite **THE SAME PERSON.** Each relationship has a special personality that goes with it.

The important thing is to realize that it's the relationships in your life that make life valuable, beautiful, and exhilarating.

For example, when Sue first joined the youth group, she was a loner, shy, and rarely spoke. But several others offered her friendship, and soon they were hanging out together. Sue built happy, strong relationships with these others, and they became very important to her. At the end of the first year, Sue sent each of her close friends a card that said, "Thanks for hanging in there with me this past year. You have made everything worth it, the good and the bad. I love you, and I'll never forget you."

In response, her friends threw a party for Sue. They told her how glad they were to have her in their lives. SUE BLOSSOMED. She continued meeting people and overcame her shyness. Eventually, Sue became one of the most popular leaders the youth group ever had—all because a few of the youth group members went out of their way to get to know a shy loner. Not only did they help change Sue's life, they changed their own lives and were rewarded with a lifelong friend.

Good Relationships Build on One Another Like Bricks

How much do you value others? Do you see what impact they have on your life? Do you see the impact you have on theirs?

Good relationships are like bricks on the foundation of a house. When they're in place and solid, it's not easy to knock that house down.

Give That Encouraging Word

How do you build great relationships? Let me offer you some pieces of wisdom I've gathered over the years.

First, learn to encourage others. Do you care about the people you're leading? If you do, then you will not withhold kind, good words from them when they're doing something well. Refuse to be a complainer. Let everyone know that whatever comes out of your mouth, it will be good.

People want to feel valued. You can give them value by many simple kinds of encouragement, such as . . .

☐ Telling them they did a good job

☐ Expressing appreciation for their attitudes

☐ Mentioning something important to them

☐ Reminding them how much they've improved in an area

Such encouragements can make a person's day, week, or year! Think of how encouraged you are when someone says something positive about something you've done. I always appreciate people who go out of their way to tell me something positive about a book I wrote or a message I preached. I savor such comments. So will you.

Our Differences Make Life Interesting

Always remember that it's the differences among us that make life exciting. If everyone looked like the latest movie star, or sang like the latest rock star, what a boring world it would be. But the fact that we're all different, with different talents, abilities, looks, preferences, and so on, is what makes life fascinating.

Team Player or Dream Breaker?

Carrie had a way of uniting everyone when they worked on a mission together. Just the right words, just the right tweaks here and there from her reminded everyone of the need to work together.

Brad, on the other hand, had the unhappy distinction of almost always ruining things for everyone. His put-downs, complaints, and general bad attitude made everyone feel it wasn't worth it.

> PEOPLE TEND TO BECOME WHAT THE MOST IMPORTANT PEOPLE IN THEIR LIVES THINK THEY WILL BECOME.

One day the youth pastor decided to use Carrie to teach Brad a lesson in team playing. He put them in a debate situation in which **BRAD HAD TO DEFEND** the youth group's dream of going into the community and working with the poor. Carrie had to show all the reasons it couldn't be done. The debate went like this:

Brad: "Well, honestly, I think it would help kids a lot."

Carrie: "I don't think it would help anyone, and it would wear us out."

Brad: "These kids don't have much. A little from us would really give them a boost, I think."

Carrie: "We just don't have that much to give away. Why waste our time?"

Brad: "But these kids deserve something better."

Carrie: "Deserve? All they deserve is hell!"

At that point, Brad got mad. "Why are you saying all these negative things, Carrie? Usually, you're for everything!"

Carrie: "I'm just doing what you always do."

Brad's jaw dropped. *"I SOUND LIKE THAT?"*

"Yesssss!" everyone in the youth group cried.

Brad hung his head a little. "I'm sorry. I'm really sorry."

At that point Carrie patted Brad on the back. "We love you, Brad. Just don't make it so hard, okay?"

From then on Brad decided to change his attitude and also to think before he spoke!

I CORINTHIANS 14:1: LOVE, THEN, IS WHAT YOU SHOULD TRY FOR.

What Do You Do with a Bad Apple?

You know it's true that one bad apple will ruin a barrel of good apples. But you can also plant a bad apple, and it'll grow into a tree just as lovely and fruitful as any that produced the good apples.

> 1 JOHN 5:16: SUPPOSE SOMEONE SEES HIS BROTHER IN CHRIST SINNING (SIN THAT DOES NOT LEAD TO ETERNAL DEATH). THAT PERSON SHOULD PRAY FOR HIS BROTHER WHO IS SINNING. THEN GOD WILL GIVE THE BROTHER LIFE.

Sometimes you will have to confront a "bad apple" before it goes bad, as Carrie did earlier. Don't flinch from the task. It's necessary for a leader to deal with people who are messing things up. Be gentle, kind, understanding, but also firm. And keep your sense of humor, too.

The Ultimate Relationship

What is the most important relationship in your life? It's your relationship with God. Without Him, you can't accomplish anything. He holds it all together like chains holding the logs on a truck.

A good question is, how can you have a great

relationship with God? What can you do to make it soar? Spend some quiet time with God. Next are several things I recommend to people who long for intimacy with God:

1. **Read God's Word.** Even if just a little every day, which will take only about fifteen minutes.

2. **Pray daily.** Keep a running list of all the people, things, events, and situations you need to pray about, and go to it often.

3. **Get involved in your youth group.** Don't just sit on the sidelines. Get involved and do something. It will make you feel part of the team.

JOHN 14:23: "IF ANY-ONE LOVES ME, THEN HE WILL OBEY MY TEACHING. MY FATHER WILL LOVE HIM, AND WE WILL COME TO HIM AND MAKE OUR HOME WITH HIM."

4. **Join your church and participate where you can.** It doesn't have to be real complicated. Start doing these things regularly, and you will find a closeness to God you will never want to lose.

9

No Grunt Work, No Glory

Laurie attended a few meetings of the youth group and usually showed up for the retreats. Eventually, she became more committed and was asked to help with the leadership. It was then that things started to go wrong.

Laurie refused to do what she considered "grunt work"—printing fliers and going door-to-door to get them out; attending planning meetings; working

> "THE LEADERSHIP INSTINCT YOU ARE BORN WITH IS THE BACK-BONE. YOU DEVELOP THE FUNNY BONE AND THE WISHBONE THAT GO WITH IT."
>
> —ELAINE AGTHER,
> CHAIRMAN,
> CHASE BANK

hard on mission trips. She thought as a leader she was "above" those things. SHE ONLY LIKED THE "GLORY" THINGS—standing up and talking in front of the group, giving her testimony in church, leading meetings, and so on.

When the next year's elections came around, she was booted off the leadership team. "But why?" she asked with tears in her eyes.

"Because you would only do the glory things," the new leader informed her. "Sometimes it's a grind, and sometimes it's glory, but our leaders have to do both—just like us."

It's an easy trap to fall into as a leader. You start to think that things should get softer now that you've "paid your dues." But leaders keep paying the dues, or they will play the blues of being kicked out!

Exercise Discipline

It comes down to discipline, finding the time and making the time for the little things a leader has to take care of. How do you develop a disciplined lifestyle? Let me offer some suggestions.

One, start now. **Don't wait.** Get involved helping with that flier or filling the punch bowl. **Be a servant.** Don't shirk your duties.

Two, start small. Don't try to get it all done at once. Take it one step at a time.

Three, apply the following seven elements to your life.

1.
Get Organized

Only you can manage your day, your week. Think through your priorities. Which should you do first? Don't skimp. Take the most important tasks and start in on them now.

2.
Go After Those Priorities, Because They Won't Go Away

Priorities are just that—the things that demand your best, your most intense scrutiny. These are the things that matter. So work on them before they start to matter to others.

3.
Put It on the Calendar, or You Will Put It Off

Do you keep a calendar? If not, you should. It's one of the easiest ways to organize your time and make sure things get done. Schedule your priorities. When will you do what?

4.
Expect Interruptions

We all have interruptions. Don't fear or roar about them. Deal with them effectively. Plan your day so that you can make decisions about interruptions without interrupting everything else.

ROMANS 8:29: AND GOD DECIDED THAT THEY WOULD BE LIKE HIS SON.

5.
Do One at a Time

A cowboy was asked how he'd been able to keep so many cattle on the range. He said, "I rope them one at a time."

You can't do more than one task at a time, so don't try. Even a juggler only actually throws one ball at a time. Work at focus, keeping on top of the things that matter, and leaving the rest to God.

6.
Figure Out What Works for You

Some people like a notebook. Others, a calendar. Whatever you choose, develop ways of doing things that fit you. Is it best to have your quiet time in the morning? Then go with that. But if you're more of an evening person, there's nothing wrong with that style. If a to-do list is your preference, use it well. Remember: The best system for you may not work for your best friend.

7.
Be Guided by Your Character, Not by Emotions

Are you the master of your feelings? When everyone's upset, can you stay in control? If not, you're letting your feelings control you. Instead, let character be your guide. Do what is right, even when it hurts.

Accountable Is Keeping a Count

One of the best ways to maintain a disciplined lifestyle is by **BEiNG ACCOUNTABLE** to someone like another leader, a friend, or your pastor or youth pastor. This is a person who will ask the hard questions:

1. Are you taking your quiet time?

2. Did you finish that job you had last week?

3. Are you on top of _____?

4. Are there any sins you're wrestling with?

When you're accountable to someone who loves you, you won't be tempted to slack off, or give up.

For example, **Manny had a problem:** waking up too late. He loved to sleep in. As a result, he often came to school tardy. His grades suffered.

''IF YOU HAVE LEARNED HOW TO DISAGREE WITHOUT BEING DISAGREEABLE, THEN YOU HAVE DISCOVERED THE SECRET OF GETTING ALONG—WHETHER IT BE BUSINESS, FAMILY RELATIONS, OR LIFE ITSELF.''

—BERNARD MELTZER,
LAW SCHOOL PROFESSOR

One day, Manny had had it. He wasn't going to sleep in ever again. It just cost him too much in time, energy, and achievement. But he knew he couldn't do it alone. So he went to Allan, his best friend, and said, "Can you keep me accountable? Will you call me every morning to help wake me up and then ask me later what time I got up, whether I had a quiet time, and so on, so I don't give up on it?" Allan agreed. And he was relentless. Every day Allan asked the same questions. But Manny found that just knowing Allan would call him each morning and ask him about those things each day would motivate him to get them done.

Finally, Allan asked, "How do I know you're not lying to me about these things?"

Manny smiled. "Because if I lie, God really smacks me!"

God wants you to succeed. So if you need someone to get into the battle with you, find

> "PEOPLE ASK THE DIF-
> FERENCE BETWEEN A
> LEADER AND A BOSS....
> THE LEADER WORKS IN
> THE OPEN, AND THE
> BOSS IN COVERT. THE
> LEADER LEADS, AND
> THE BOSS DRIVES."
>
> —THEODORE ROOSEVELT,
> TWENTY-SIXTH
> PRESIDENT
> OF THE UNITED STATES

an accountability partner. He or she could change your life.

Now you know what it takes to become a good leader. I'm confident if you follow these principles, you will see SUCCESS ON A LEVEL you never dreamed possible. God is in the business of blessing us, not making things hard or unbearable.

PHILIPPIANS 3:21: HE WILL CHANGE OUR SIMPLE BODIES AND MAKE THEM LIKE HIS OWN GLORIOUS BODY. CHRIST CAN DO THIS BY HIS POWER. WITH THAT POWER HE IS ABLE TO RULE ALL THINGS.

So prepare to be surprised, even amazed. God can do more than you've ever dreamed, if you'll do the simple things He asks.

As a young man I learned this poem. It is an appropriate way to end this book.

Ah, great it is to believe the dream,

As we stand in youth by the starry stream;

But a greater thing is to fight life through,

And say at the end, "The dream is true!"